Midnight Mushroom Coloring Book

Before you start

Thank you for choosing our coloring book.
Your support motivates us to keep creating
awesome coloring books.
Unleash your creativity and relax while you enjoy coloring
these unique mushrooms theme designs.

When Coloring

Amazon's selection of paper is most suited for colored pencils
and alcohol-based markers. When coloring with wet medium,
keep in mind to place a sheet of paper
behind the page you are coloring to prevent bleed-through.

When you finish coloring

We hope you have a memorable experience
while exploring this coloring book. Don't forget to
leave a review and share your finished pictures on Amazon.

First printing 2023

ISBN 9798374227055

COLOR TEST